D1357063

CRICKET

CRICKET

WICKETS, WIT, AND WISDOM

Compiled by Richard Knott

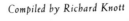

Running Press

PHILADELPHIA • LONDON

A Running Press Miniature Edition™
© 1996 by Running Press
Illustrations © 1996 Izhar Cohen
Printed in China

British Library Cataloguing-in-Publication Data
A catalogue record for this book is available from the British Library.

ISBN 1-56138-753-3

This book may be ordered by mail from the publisher.
Please include £1.00 for postage and handling.
But try your bookstore first!

Running Press Book Publishers
Cedar House
35 Chichele Road
Oxted, Surrey RH8 0AE

CONTENTS

Introduction............ 6

The Game.............. 12

The Players........... 40

Of Ashes and Tests..... 76

Extras............... 100

INTRODUCTION

Cricket is a game with a long history, cherished traditions, and a heavily populated hall of fame. Part of its magic, for spectators and players alike, is that very sense of history, the connections it makes with times long gone. It is a game of subtlety, played at its best over five days when the plot has time to unfold and twist, working towards an ultimate, but scarcely guessed at, resolution. Like other great sports, there is something highly theatrical and truly dramatic about it. The dramatic elements come from the arenas where cricket is played: the green amphitheatre, with its scattered figures in white. This is true whether the game is a Test

match played at Lord's or a village contest in
deepest Somerset or Devon—with the outfield
dense with daisies sloping towards a winding
country lane and a thatched inn beyond the
cricket field's fence. But the game itself transcends
the field of play: it can be graceful, brutal,
passionate, cruel sometimes—all within
one summer's day. It is an intelligent game,
where reflection and shrewd calculation repay
themselves. It is instinctive too:
the moment when a batsman
chooses to hook or duck,
glance fine or clip through
midwicket, happens so fast.
For a batsman,
the game can

be over in the blinking of an eye. For a bowler, the game is about perseverance, guile, stamina, and unbounded optimism.

There is one last feature which sets the game apart: the people who play it. Most professional cricketers play cricket day in, day out, throughout the summer, and then, once the autumn comes, they slip into relative obscurity. It's a kind of hibernation. In the season, a day's rain might mean a game of cards or the crossword in the pavilion, but may be welcomed as a day away from the intense concentration and unrelenting physical demand. Perhaps it is that which prompts the laconic camaraderie which characterises cricketers. Cricketers, by and large, like each other—they laugh a lot and expect to share a leisurely beer or two after the day's play is over. They are often good with words—all that time for reflection standing in the deep.

The words which follow are testimony to the wit, intelligence, companionship, and rivalry of players over many years. These quotations from good old pros, cricket-loving playwrights, actors, novelists, among others, capture what it is that makes cricket the most humane of games. It should be read for best effect on cold winter nights with a glass of malt whisky in the hours before the ball-by-ball commentary starts from the other side of the world, or in a deck-chair on the boundary edge with half an eye on the game out in the sun-baked middle.

The Game

Explaining the rules of cricket is an excellent test for high-powered brains.

JOHN MAJOR
PRIME MINISTER

You have two sides, one out in the field
and one in. Each man that's in the side
that's in goes out and when he's out he
comes in and the next man goes in until
he's out. When they are all out the side
that's out comes in and the side that's
been in goes out and tries to get those
coming in out. Sometimes you get men
still in and not out. When both sides
have been in and out, including the not
outs—that's the end of the game.

ANONYMOUS

The laws of cricket tell of the English
love of compromise between a particular
freedom and a general orderliness,
or legality.

NEVILLE CARDUS
CRICKET WRITER

There is no talk that is as good as cricket talk, when memory sharpens . . . and the old happy days of burned out Junes revive. . . .

ANDREW LANG
WRITER

The instant, one-day game is rather like a one-act play, whereas a five-day Test corresponds to an Elizabethan five-act drama with its swift reversals of fortune and cumulative tension.

MICHAEL BILLINGTON
THEATRE CRITIC, THE GUARDIAN

A rural cricket match in buttercup time, seen and heard through the trees; it is surely the loveliest scene in England and the most disarming sound. From the ranks of the unseen dead, forever passing along our country lanes on their eternal journey, the Englishmen fall out for a moment to look over the gate of the cricket field and smile.

SIR JAMES BARRIE
WRITER

The cricket field itself was a mass of daisies and buttercups and dandelions, tall grasses and purple vetches and thistle-down, and great clumps of dark-red sorrel, except, of course, for the oblong patch in the centre—mown, rolled, watered—and a smooth, shining, emerald of grass, the Pride of Fordenden, the Wicket.

A. G. MACDONNELL
FROM ENGLAND, THEIR ENGLAND

How can I ever go back to an indoor job? I'm like a Dartmoor pony. I've smelt the summer turf and felt it under my feet.

JACK DAVEY
FORMER GLOUCESTERSHIRE PROFESSIONAL

Lord's on a warm day, with a bottle, a
mixed bag of sandwiches, and a couple
of spare pipes in a despatch case, and I
don't care who is playing whom. Cricket
is the only game I can enjoy without
taking sides.

A. A. MILNE
WRITER

. . . the sound of cricket bats: pick, pack, pock, puck: like drops of water in a fountain falling softly in the brimming bowl.

JAMES JOYCE
FROM A PORTRAIT OF THE ARTIST
AS A YOUNG MAN

They call it a team game, but in fact it's the loneliest game of all.

JOHN ARLOTT
CRICKET WRITER AND COMMENTATOR

Cricket is the only game where you are playing against eleven of the other side and ten of your own.

G. H. HARDY
MATHEMATICIAN

Personally, I have always
looked on cricket as organised loafing.

WILLIAM TEMPLE
FORMER ARCHBISHOP OF CANTERBURY

First class cricket has for years excelled all other games because of the scope and opportunity it allows for the exhibition of personal art, because of its appeal as a spectacle delightful to see and be present at on a summer day, rain or no rain. . . . There can be no summer in this land without cricket. . . . Cricket, as I know and love it, is part of that holiday time which is the Englishman's heritage—a playtime in a homely countryside.

NEVILLE CARDUS
CRICKET WRITER

When the cricket season was
over I felt a deep sadness. It was
like the end of harvest.

ALISON UTTLEY
WRITER

Graveney may have disappointed some cricketers by playing in Graveney's way, but he has adorned cricket. In an age preoccupied with accountancy, he has given the game warmth and colour and inspiration beyond the tally of the scorebook. He has been of the orchard rather than the forest, blossom susceptible to frost. . . .

J. M. KILBURN
CRICKET WRITER, YORKSHIRE POST

I have often thought of how much better a life I would have had, what a better man I would have been, how much healthier an existence I would have led, if I had been a cricketer instead of an actor.

SIR LAURENCE OLIVIER
ACTOR

When he was at school his headmaster caught him climbing over a wall and asked what he was up to. . . . The boy said he was bored with class and thought he might pop down to St Helen's and watch Glamorgan at cricket. 'Dylan,' said the head, 'that is very wrong of you. Very wrong indeed.' And then as he walked away, he half turned and called out: 'I hope someone catches you.'

TIM HEALD,
ABOUT THE POET DYLAN THOMAS

The captain used my head as a desk to write on, and I experienced much more spiritual elevation than I felt at fourteen from the hand of a bishop at confirmation.

GRAHAM GREENE,
AS AN AUTOGRAPH-HUNTING ADOLESCENT

Bowled well against Tonbridge but did
nothing else. Does not use his head at
all. A poor bat and a very slack field.

THE CRICKET EXPLOITS OF
P. G. WODEHOUSE, AS DESCRIBED
IN HIS SCHOOL MAGAZINE

Cricket is basically baseball on valium.

ROBIN WILLIAMS
ACTOR

There's a breathless
hush in the Close tonight,
Ten to make and the match to win—
A bumping pitch and a blinding light
An hour to play and the last man in.

SIR HENRY NEWBOULT
POET

THE PLAYERS

He'd be keeping wicket all day in
Sydney, ninety-five in the shade, and
never miss a thing. . . . Like the rest of
us he would stagger off the field, have
a bath, get dressed, have a drink, sit
down at the piano in the hotel, and start
to play. He was ready for the evening.
That's what you need on tour.

LEN HUTTON,
YORKSHIRE AND CAPTAIN OF ENGLAND,
ABOUT ENGLAND WICKET-KEEPER
GODFREY EVANS

To us cricket had no season. Any old
time and any old place was good
enough. Some of our most exciting
matches were played after darkness had
set in, played in an underground passage
with a candle behind the wicket at one
end, another behind the bowler, and one
in the middle of the pitch. I'm not sure
that this was not the most difficult
wicket upon which I have ever played.

GILBERT 'THE CROUCHER' JESSOP
GLOUCESTERSHIRE AND ENGLAND

On the day I can't play cricket anymore, I'll do as them Romans did—I'll get into a 'ot bath and cut mi ruddy throat!

CECIL PARKIN
LANCASHIRE AND ENGLAND

Plenty of bowlers have taken 1,000 wickets, but none 999!

'BOMBER' WELLS,
GLOUCESTERSHIRE.
ON CHOOSING THE APPROPRIATE
MOMENT TO RETIRE FROM THE GAME

Concentration. Every ball is for me
the first ball, whether my score is 0 or
200. And I never visualise the possibility
of *anybody* getting me out.

SIR DON BRADMAN
AUSTRALIAN BATSMAN

Cricket is full of theorists who can ruin your game in no time.

IAN BOTHAM
ENGLAND ALL ROUNDER

On Friday I watched J. M. Brearley
directing his fieldsmen very carefully.
He then looked up at the sun and made
a gesture which seemed to indicate
that it should move a little squarer.
Who is this man?

S. A. NICHOLAS
FROM A LETTER TO <u>THE GUARDIAN</u>

He had no style and yet he was all style. He had three strokes for every ball.

C. B. FRY,
ABOUT VICTOR TRUMPER,
AUSTRALIAN BATSMAN

. . . in the years 1910 and 1911 I had
fifty-one innings, with ten not outs, and
an average of nineteen. This I consider
quite a creditable record for a poet.

SIEGFRIED SASSOON
POET

Look at the old man; old enough to be
my father, damned nearly blind and
batting better from memory than I shall
ever do.

ANONYMOUS,
ABOUT HAMPSHIRE'S PHIL MEAD
BATTING AFTER RETIREMENT IN
A WARTIME CHARITY MATCH

Asked to sum up his philosophy of cricket, he said: 'Never bowl your granny a full toss, even on her birthday.'

MICHAEL PARKINSON,
ABOUT BILL ALLEY, AUSTRALIAN-BORN
SOMERSET CRICKETER AND UMPIRE

Don't show him your googly, top
spinner, flipper, or anything else except
those gentle dobbing leggers outside
off stump.

AUSTRALIAN CAPTAIN TO THE THEN-
UNKNOWN SHANE WARNE ON HIS FIRST
TOUR OF ENGLAND

There is no such thing as a crisis in cricket, only the next ball.

W. G. GRACE
GLOUCESTERSHIRE AND ENGLAND

There was a young cleric called Glover
Who bowled twenty-one wides in one over
Which had never been done
By a clergyman's son
On a Thursday, in August, at Dover.

LIMERICK ON VILLAGE
CRICKET CLUB NOTICEBOARD

None of us likes it, but some of us shows it more than others.

MAURICE LEYLAND,
YORKSHIRE AND ENGLAND,
ABOUT FAST BOWLING

Whenever he hit the stumps a broad smile came across his face which he tried to conceal. It would not interest him if somebody was *caught* off his bowling.

ARTHUR CARR,
ABOUT HAROLD LARWOOD, ENGLAND
FAST BOWLER

Ray Lindwall never bowled a bouncer at me. He said that if he couldn't bowl out a number nine then he oughtn't to be playing for Australia.

JIM LAKER
SURREY AND ENGLAND

I felt as if I ought to fetch him back and tell him that I hadn't meant that sort of ball at all.

J. G. W DAVIES,
KENT AND CAMBRIDGE UNIVERSITY, AFTER
BOWLING THE GREAT DON BRADMAN FOR
0 WITH AN OFF BREAK THAT DIDN'T TURN

It's like trying to bowl to God on concrete.

R. C. ROBERTSON-GLASGOW,
ABOUT BOWLING TO
SIR JACK HOBBS AT THE OVAL

You know, I always had snuff in my pocket when I was bowling. I often used to take a pinch of it on the field in Australia. It used to freshen me up. And it's much better for you than cigarettes.

HAROLD LARWOOD
NOTTINGHAMSHIRE AND ENGLAND

'I allow only one batsman to cock a snoop at me, and that's the "Old Man" (W. G. Grace), put it down young feller.' The batsman declined to put his foot down, so Kortright landed his fastest yorker on the toe cap; and the young feller was then solicitously helped from the field.

NEVILLE CARDUS
CRICKET WRITER

Tha' knows one thing about cricket: tha'
can't put in what God left out. Tha' sees
two kinds of cricketers, them that uses a
bat as if they are shovelling muck and
them that plays proper, and like as not
God showed both of them how to play.

WILFRED RHODES
YORKSHIRE AND ENGLAND

He seemed to walk out to bat with a
Union Jack trailing behind him.

WALLY GROUT,
AUSTRALIAN WICKET-KEEPER,
ABOUT KEN BARRINGTON, ENGLISH BATSMAN

Kid yourself it's Sunday, Rev, and keep
your hands together.

FRED TRUEMAN,
YORKSHIRE FAST BOWLER,
TO HIS ENGLAND COLLEAGUE THE REV.
DAVID SHEPPARD (NOW BISHOP OF
LIVERPOOL) AFTER A SUCCESSION
OF DROPPED CATCHES

There was all summer in a stroke by Woolley, and he batted as it is sometimes shown in dreams.

R. C. ROBERTSON-GLASGOW
FROM CRICKET PRINTS

Cricket is peculiar in that despite being a big team game, the batsmen leave the field individually, taking their bow for success or hanging their heads after failure, in a way reminiscent of an opera house.

LORD FORTE
CRICKET FAN

That ball went through Boycott's defence like a bullet through a hole in a Henry Moore.

JOHN ARLOTT
CRICKET WRITER AND COMMENTATOR

There be an epidemic on this field, but I can tell youse it ain't catching!

WALTER MEAD.
ESSEX AND ENGLAND BOWLER.
TO HIS BUTTER-FINGERED TEAMMATES

OF ASHES
AND TESTS

Basil D'Oliveira, England all rounder: The ultimate thing in life is to play for England.

John Snow, Sussex and England pace bowler: My friend, the ultimate thing in life is death.

Pray God, that a professional
should never captain England.

LORD HAWKE
YORKSHIRE AND ENGLAND

Still the game is essentially Anglo-Saxon.
Foreigners have rarely, very rarely
imitated us . . . no cricket club have we
ever heard dieted with frogs, sour crout,
or macaroni.

THE REVEREND JAMES PYCROFT
VICTORIAN CRICKET WRITER

To watch the West Indian captain laying
into the demoralised English bowlers
is like watching Martina Navratilova
playing Little Orphan Annie!

TONY COZIER,
WEST INDIAN CRICKET COMMENTATOR,
ABOUT VIV RICHARDS

I should like to state that my eyesight
and concentration are almost as good
now as when I had the honour of playing
for England along with my old partner
Sir J. B. Hobbs. I must confess I find it
difficult to think I have proceeded
through traffic lights at red.

HERBERT SUTCLIFFE,
YORKSHIRE AND ENGLAND, AGED 73
(HE WAS FINED 20 SHILLINGS)

Funny match, Lancashire and Yorkshire, two teams meet at beginning and we say 'Good Morning'; then we never speak again for three days, except to appeal.

ROY KILNER
YORKSHIRE AND ENGLAND

Gooch and his black moustache surely
saw service in England's old imperial
wars, defending Rorke's Drift and march-
ing up the Khyber Pass.

GEOFFREY MOORHOUSE,
ABOUT GRAHAM GOOCH,
ESSEX AND ENGLAND

It's all right, but what we need in Yorkshire-Lancashire matches is *no umpires*—and fair cheatin' all around.

MAURICE LEYLAND
YORKSHIRE AND ENGLAND

Bill Andrews, debutant professional, Somerset: Mr Young, am I the worst cricketer ever to play first class cricket?

Tom Young, senior pro, Somerset: No, son, there is one worse who plays for Glamorgan.

The only time I've seen an Australian walk is when he's run out of petrol.

BARRY RICHARDS
HAMPSHIRE AND SOUTH AFRICA

When we spoke of literary figures, we spoke of Englishmen. But when we spoke of cricket, we spoke of our own. . . . No Australian had written *Paradise Lost*, but Bradman had made 100 before lunch at Lord's.

THOMAS KENEALLY,
AUSTRALIAN WRITER, RECALLING
HIS SCHOOL DAYS

I couldn't wait to have a crack at 'em (the English). I thought: 'Stuff that stiff upper lip, brat. Let's see how stiff it is when it's split.'

JEFF THOMSON
AUSTRALIAN FAST BOWLER

I have always fantasised about cricket.
Even now, on sleepless nights, I can
dismiss the entire Australian eleven for
a dozen runs.

DONALD PLEASANCE
ACTOR

After lunch the Australians, arrogant, jocular, muscular, larking down the pavilion steps. They waited, hurling the ball about, eight feet tall. Two shapes behind the pavilion glass. Frozen before emerging a split second. Hutton and Compton. We knew them to be the two greatest English batsmen.

HAROLD PINTER,
ABOUT THE 1948 AUSTRALIANS

A cricket tour in Australia would be a most delightful period in one's life if one was deaf.

HAROLD LARWOOD
NOTTINGHAMSHIRE AND ENGLAND

D

on't swat those poor flies, Mr Jardine. They're the only friends you've got in Australia.

Australia faced a deficit of 375 runs on the first innings. With Laker rampant, it was a lost cause. Ian Johnson, the Australian captain, tried a pep talk. He told his team: 'We can fight back. We need guts and determination. We can still save this match.' Keith Miller was studying a racing guide at the time. He looked up: 'Bet you 6–4 we can't,' he said.

MICHAEL PARKINSON
CRICKET WRITER

At one end stocky Jessop stands
The human caterpult,
Who wrecks the roofs of distant towns
When set in his assault.

BY AN AMERICAN RHYMESTER,
AFTER GILBERT JESSOP PLAYED AGAINST
THE GENTLEMEN OF PHILADELPHIA

EXTRAS

It's a funny kind of month, October. For the really keen cricket fan, it's when you realise that your wife left you in May.

DENNIS NORDEN
COMEDIAN AND SCRIPTWRITER

Had this country been ruled in its pomp
and in its prime by a monarch who had
played Test Match cricket, opened the
innings for her country at Headingley,
been struck in the ribs by Spofforth at
The Oval, smashed in the teeth by
Gregory at Old Trafford, bitten on the
buttocks by the groundsman's ferrets at
Trent Bridge, is it conceivable that
Britain should be in its present desperate
plight with women newsreaders on the
moving television screens and threatened
centre-page pin-ups of Brian Johnston in
Wisden's Almanack?

PETER TINNISWOOD
FROM TALES FROM THE LONG ROOM

A loving wife is better than making 50 at cricket or even 99; beyond that I will not go.

SIR JAMES BARRIE
WRITER

I don't know if I prefer Rog to have
a good innings or a bad one: if it's a
good one, he relives it in bed, shot by
shot, and if it's a bad one he actually
replays the shots until he gets it right.
He can make a really good innings last
all winter.

RICHARD HARRIS
FROM <u>OUTSIDE EDGE</u>

If Beethoven had been employed by the Test and County Cricket Board, he would have been pensioned off with the reference: 'It's all very well coming out

with a concerto every now and again, but we'd have employed him a good deal longer if the wretched boy had practised his scales more often.

MARTIN JOHNSON,
ABOUT DAVID GOWER, FORMER
ENGLAND CAPTAIN

CRICKET ···

Say, when does it begin?

GROUCHO MARX
QUOTED AT LORD'S, UPON SEEING
HIS FIRST GAME — FIVE MINUTES AFTER
THE GAME HAD STARTED

108

I floated out through the Long Room.
People were looking at me. I could hear
them muttering 'Who's this old grey
bugger?' as I walked past. Tommo stood
with his hands on his hips. I said 'Good
morning, Tommo.' He said, 'Bloody hell,
who've we got here? Groucho Marx?'

DAVID STEELE
ENGLAND

There's no point hitting me there; there's nothing in it.

DEREK RANDALL,
ENGLAND BATSMAN,
AFTER BEING HIT ON THE HEAD
BY A DENNIS LILLEE BOUNCER

Jamaican judge: I have to tell you, gentlemen, that Boyce is dismissed.

Defence Counsel: But m'lud, my client's name is Bryce.

Judge: Ah, quite so, but I thought you would like to know the latest Test score from Sabina Park.

A lady wrote to me saying how much she had enjoyed our commentaries but that I ought to be more careful, as we had a lot of young listeners. She asked me if I realised what I said . . . as Michael Holding was bowling to Peter Willey. She told me that I had said: 'The bowler's holding the batsman's willy.'

BRIAN JOHNSTON
CRICKET COMMENTATOR

Ｉt's perfectly apparent that
your mother was an actress.

MIKE BREARLEY TO MARK NICHOLAS
OF HAMPSHIRE, AFTER NICHOLAS HAD
BEEN HIT BY A BALL FROM JEFF THOMSON

Hey Willis! Your dad wanted a daughter and your ma wanted a son. They're both happy!

AUSTRALIAN FAN TO
ENGLAND FAST BOWLER
BOB WILLIS

When you play in a match, be sure not
to forget to pay a little attention to the
umpire. First of all inquire after his
health, then say what a good player his
father was, and finally present him with a
brace of birds or rabbits.

GEORGE PARR
NOTTINGHAMSHIRE AND ENGLAND

As a bowler delivered the ball the umpire ejaculated 'Brrr' and, after a pause, added, 'I beg your pardon, I meant to say "no-ball", but I dropped my teeth.'

LETTER TO THE *TIMES*, 1935

The umpire asks me to tell you that he is very sorry, but he felt his arm going up and couldn't stop it.

INDIAN OFFICIAL TO MIKE BREARLEY

It might have been more, but the umpire, Bill Reeves, admitted afterwards that he'd given me out lbw to Jim Parks because he was desperate for a pee.

DENIS COMPTON,
MIDDLESEX AND ENGLAND,
DESCRIBING HIS FIRST INNINGS
FOR MIDDLESEX

Not out, not out. It's a sixpenny crowd,
Saturday gate, can't disappoint 'em.
Near thing but not near enough for
the occasion.

UMPIRE IGNORING
INCONTESTABLE EVIDENCE THAT
GILBERT JESSOP WAS RUN OUT
(JESSOP DULY SCORED A HUNDRED)

April: This is the time of the year when the sentimental cricketer withdraws his bat tenderly from its winter bed and croons over it, as if it were a Stradivarius or a shoulder of mutton.

R. C. ROBERTSON-GLASGOW
CRICKET WRITER

Eh, Brearley! Why don't y'pin it back on w'a six-inch nail!

TRENT BRIDGE FAN TO THE ENGLAND
SKIPPER WHEN HIS HELMET FELL OFF

I enjoyed it, but if I go back again I will
wear a tin hat.

LAURIE LEE, AFTER BEING HIT ON THE
HEAD BY A BOTTLE AT THE SYDNEY
CRICKET GROUND

A beautiful
game which is battle and service
and sport and art.

DOUGLAS JARDINE
ENGLAND CAPTAIN